ANGELS OF POMPEII

Porta a Pompèi

Untitled Angel (The Muse)

ANGELS

OF POMPEII

Photographs by Stephen Brigidi

Poetry by Robert Bly

BALLANTINE BOOKS / NEW YORK

Poetry and Foreword copyright © 1991 by Robert Bly
Photographs and Afterword copyright © 1991 by Stephen Brigidi
Chronology copyright © 1991 by Deborah Jones

Library of Congress Cataloging - in - Publication Data
Bly. Robert.
Angels of Pompeii/photographs by Stephen Brigidi:
poetry by Robert Bly. — 1st ed.
p. cm.
ISBN 0 - 345 - 37741 - 9
1. Angels — Poetry. 2. Pompeii (Ancient city) — Poetry. 3. Mural
painting and decoration — Italy — Pompeii (Ancient city) 4. Angels
in art. I. Brigidi. Stephen. II. Title.
PS3552.L9A82   1992
811'.54 — dc20   91 - 58181
                    CIP

Designed by Malcolm Grear Designers

Manufactured in the United States of America

First Edition: January 1992
10 9 8 7 6 5 4 3 2 1

Parete Sezione a Pompèi

FOREWORD

Stephen Brigidi sent me these photographs two years ago, and I liked them more and more as I lived with them. These shapes or figures at first seem so like angels, then like souls whose buried bodies still lie beneath the street. We know the shapes are the figures that constantly floated through the Roman imagination, carrying their private grief and their public hints of earlier gods and goddesses. Stephen Brigidi has photographed them brilliantly, so the gods and goddesses stand out from the brown or blue walls of desire. Some of the poems I have put next to them are old poems of mine that go back twenty years which I finished for this collection; others are new.

ROBERT BLY

Parete d'Ostia Antica

Parete con Cuore, Pompèi

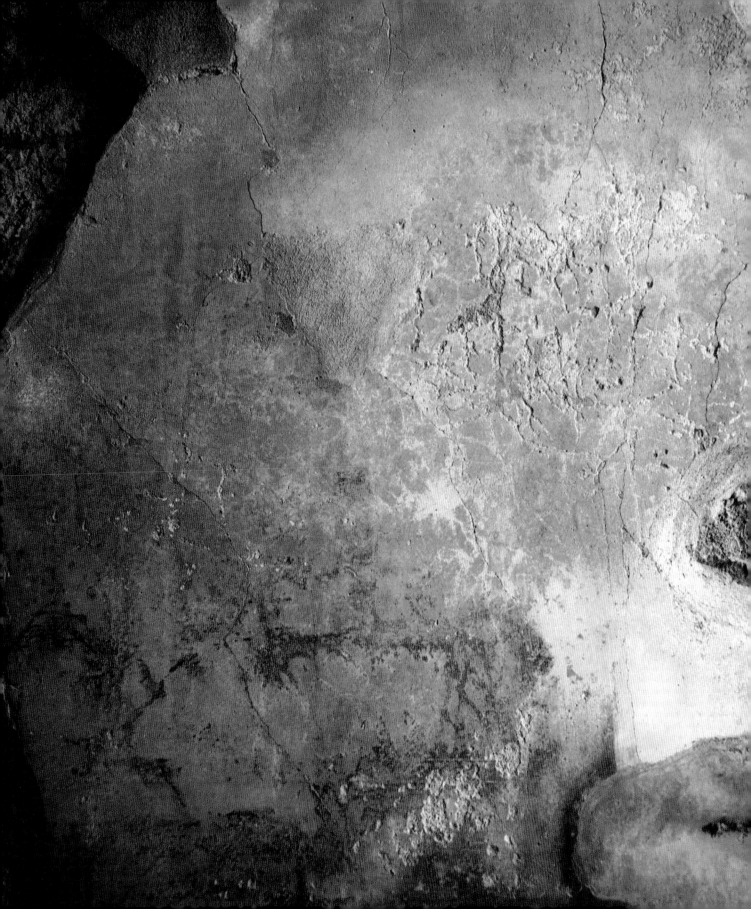

Who is this who is constantly coming closer?

It is the man in the ship's hold.

It is what the body knows, what it holds.

And this one who is constantly coming closer,

Ah, that is the spontaneous, mercurial one,

Imprisoned in the cedar root or the mustard seed.

He is no one we know: he is not Jehovah,

Or an obedient ermine-caparisoned king.

He is one nearer than near, closer than fingernails.

Are we all then religious? It must be so.

We know him, we see him, we hold him every day.

He is the one constantly coming closer.

Early in the morning the hermit wakes,

Hearing the roots of the fir tree stir beneath his floor.

Someone is there. That strength buried

In earth carries up the summer world.

When a man loves a woman, he nourishes her.

Dancers strew the lawns with the light of their feet.

When a woman loves the earth, she nourishes it.

Earth nourishes what no one can see.

Muro. Ostia Antica

After writing poems all day.

I go off to see the moon in the pines.

Far in the woods I set down against a pine.

The moon has her porches turned to face the light.

But the deep part of her house is in darkness.

A PRIVATE FALL

1   Motes of haydust rise and fall

With slow and grave steps,

Like servants who dance in the yard

Because some prince has been born.

2   What has been born? The winter.

Then the Egyptians were right.

Everything wants a chance to begin,

To die in the clear fall air.

3   Each leaf sinks and goes down

When we least expect it.

We glance toward the window for

Something has caught our eye.

4   It's possible autumn is a tomb

Out of which a child is born.

We feel a secret joy

And we tell no one!

It was midsummer. Something was waiting

Or being waited for.

I threw oatstraw bales in the afternoon.

And then washed chaff from my hair.

In my dream last night I visited the ocean.

It was a far off place where the dead live

Hanging from trees. like the giant boas.

The dead hung exhausted but sleeping.

Toward dawn a cube of earth stood

Near me on a blue cloth. a cube

Of grief. Each time a man nudges it

With his shoulders. he goes one step higher.

Muro a Pompèi

Parete d'Ercolano

Muro d'Pompèi

Parete Azzurro. Ercolano

What is sorrow for? It is a storehouse set

On rocks for wheat, barley, corn, and tears.

One steps to the door on a round stone.

The storehouse feeds all the birds of sorrow.

And I say to myself: Will you have

Sorrow at last? Go on, be cheerful in autumn,

Be stoic, yes, be tranquil, calm,

Or in the valley of sorrows spread your wings.

Dettaglio del Parete, Ostia Antica

I found you floating in the night sky,

Sword-belted, gleaming above the farm:

A star man hunting wild stars,

Noticeable most when the moon is hidden.

When people like us look up to the stars,

They cannot tell what being is down

At their feet, what gives or is given,

What suffering shape may crouch there.

The Hunter drops his eyes to follow the tracks

Of his dogs, who follow the hare. But we,

Preferring — rightly — to know the stars do not

See the shape that dies to feed us.

A HOME IN DARK GRASS

In the deep fall, the body awakes,

And we find lions on the seashore —

Nothing to fear.

The wind rises; water is born,

Spreading white tomb-clothes on a rocky shore,

Drawing us up

From the bed of the land.

It is not our job to remain whole.

We came to lose our leaves

Like the trees, and be born again,

Drawing up from the great roots.

So men captured by the Moors

Wake in the cold ocean

Air, living a second life.

That we should learn of poverty and rags,

And taste the weed of Dillinger,

And swim in the sea,

Not always walking on dry land,

And, dancing, find in the trees a savior,

A home in dark grass,

And nourishment in death.

Muro Sezione, Pompèi

Parete. Ercolano

Muro. Ostia Antica

AFTERWORD

My attraction to Pompeii began as a mild fascination with archaeology and history with my first visit there in 1972. This initial experience affected me deeply, causing more trips to that famed site in southern Italy during the seventies. What began to occur during these sojourns was a feeling of *bonding*, of a force at work within, linking me to my ancestry. My photography at Pompeii was directed toward the colored and fragmented walls of decay like some magnetic attachment. I would occasionally offer a guard at the ancient city some incentive to show me still another "off-limits" area. The angels were a discovery that stopped me long enough to accept their light and their heat. In retrospect, I must have asked for some kind of personal blessing that day in August 1978.

At first this work lay dormant within my larger inventory of Italian images, but by 1985 I began to experiment with the printing of the angels. I realized their potential as a small body of work which I preferred as a suite of pictures. It was never an issue that some of the figures did not bear wings; as an artist and as a man, I saw them as angels. The angel's great power became clear to me as I began to appreciate their great archetypal presence, and observed how their mysterious nature inspired many with whom I had shared the work. I felt that the *poetry* of the angels could best be communicated when combined with the response of another artist who perceived the angel's message much the same as I.

Robert Bly was an artist I knew from his many writings over the years. I sent him the angels (no longer claiming them as my own) for his reaction. And react he did with powerful words to make the marriage happen. Bly's poems inspired by the images and sensations of the figures produced a creative joining. This collection of words and pictures has become a dual body, our shared dialogue in appreciation.

STEPHEN BRIGIDI 1991

Facciata con Colonne. Pompèi

Dettaglio del Muro, Pompèi

CHRONOLOGY *Deborah Jones*

8th Century B.C.

The city of Pompeii in the Campania region of Italy is first settled by the Oscans, descendents of the neolithic inhabitants of Campania. The original 24-acre settlement is built on a prehistoric lava flow overlooking the river mouth. Greeks from Cumae compete with Estruscans from Capua to colonize Pompeii.

6th – 5th Century B.C.

With the defeat of the Etruscans, Greek influence flourishes, and Pompeii's size increases to a 160-acre settlement.

290 B.C. – 80 B.C.

There is continuous civil strife after the Samnite wars; however, the Romans' triumphant advances turn Pompeii into a major agricultural and commercial port.

200 B.C. – 60 B.C.

The First or "Masonry" Style of wall painting originates. Using various color contrasts of marble and alabaster, this style emphasizes the solid qualities of the walls it adorns. Artists are considered manual laborers and rarely sign their work.

60 B.C. – 20 A.D.

The "Architectural" or Second Style of wall painting develops. It employs simulated architectural columns and cornices, creating an illusion of space and light on the main wall surface.

At this time, traditional religion is one of personal mythic belief and practice, satisfying everyday needs. While the great gods of Olympus and the Mystery religions symbolize the well-being of the Roman state, people turn to their household shrines of local saints for help in facing the hazards of the world.

27 B.C. – 54 A.D.

The Third Style of wall painting emerges while the Architectural style is still in use. It concentrates on extreme elegance and vivid colors, depicting decorative garlands of flowers and vines on a single monochromatic background.

Pompeii's rapid growth and change allows a free atmosphere where wealthy philhellenes indulge in excesses of pleasure and exhibitionism.

62 A.D.

A violent earthquake badly damages much of the city.

20 A.D. – 79 A.D.

The Fourth Style of wall painting evolves, portraying architectural patterns enlivened with mythological themes. Many houses are painted with elaborate picture galleries depicting emotional faces, mentors of the inhabitants, initiation rites, gods and goddesses, and mythological beasts. These depictions allowed legends to be related within secular life. The angels are painted during this period.

24 August 79 A.D.

16,000 out of 20,000 inhabitants of Pompeii perish as Mount Vesuvius, previously thought to be a dormant volcano, erupts without warning, burying (and preserving) Pompeii, as well as nearby Herculaneum and Stabaie, beneath 20 feet of volcanic debris.

1709

Workmen digging an irrigation tunnel accidentally come upon the first of the ancient city artifacts, prompting the ruling nobility of Naples to scavenge haphazardly in the ruins for treasure.

1808 – 1815

Joachim Murat, king of Naples, institutes the first scientifically conducted excavations of Pompeii.

1860 – 1875

Giuseppe Fiorelli, chief excavator at Pompeii, introduces the systematic approach of nomenclature (still in use today) and develops a technique of injecting plaster into hollows, thus creating a method of negative casting.

1924 – 1961

Amadeo Maiuri, a distinguished archeologist, continues systematic, street-by-street excavations in the buried cities, restoring each object to the place it occupied at the instant of the eruption.

1972

Stephen Brigidi first visits Pompeii where he makes documentary-style photographs of the area and ruins.

1975

Drawn by the colors and textures of the interior and exterior ruin walls, Brigidi returns to Pompeii to photograph them.

1978

Brigidi travels with Fulbright support through southern Italy, stopping in Ercolano (modern Herculaneum) and Pompeii for more extensive photographing of the walls and ruins. The angels are discovered.

1980

Although Mount Vesuvius is quiet, a severe earthquake strikes southern Italy leaving Pompeii shell-shocked. The exposed wall paintings continue to fade and decay as funds are unavailable to maintain such a large monument.

1985

Brigidi produces "The Angel Suite," an artist's edition of eight cibachrome prints of the angel photographs.

1991

Collaboration of Stephen Brigidi and Robert Bly on "Angels of Pompeii."

AUTHOR'S NOTES

Angels of Pompeii is the result of a collaboration
beginning with Stephen Brigidi and Robert Bly.
It was the creative design work of Malcolm Grear that
brought about the successful integration of photographs
and poems. Pat Appleton and Nadine Flowers were
essential parts of the design team who labored to make
the book possible. and David Klein of Palm Press
contributed his expertise in producing the dye transfer
prints. Finally. the participation of Ballantine Books
with Joelle Delbourgo and Fred Dodnick complete this
collaborative effort.

Angels of Pompeii
designed by Malcolm Grear Designers
was typeset in Bodoni and
printed on Karma paper.

An artist's edition of Angels of Pompeii has been
published as a portfolio limited to twenty-five copies
and ten artist's proofs. The poems are set in letterpress
Bodoni type and paired with archival dye transfer
prints of the angels. The collection is matted on fine
Stonehenge paper and contained in a custom basswood
case covered with french marbled leaves and an Italian
Canapetta linen. The portfolio has been designed by
Malcolm Grear and published by The Bristol Workshops
in Photography. 474 Thames Street, Bristol. Rhode
Island 02809.

Parete a Pompèi